why birds migrate

by Julian May

illustrated by Chet Reneson

why birds migrate

Holiday House · New York

YELLOW
WARBLER

Several million years ago, there
was no winter in our land. It was
warm all through the year, and birds
lived everywhere.

INDIGO
BUNTING

REDWING
BLACKBIRD

SCARLET
TANAGER

BLACKBIRD

ROBIN

They found food all through the year.
It was never too cold to raise young.
Birds could have several families
each year.

BOBWHITE
QUAIL

During these early times, birds probably did not travel much. Why should they? Everything they needed for a good life was close to home.

YELLOW
WARBLER

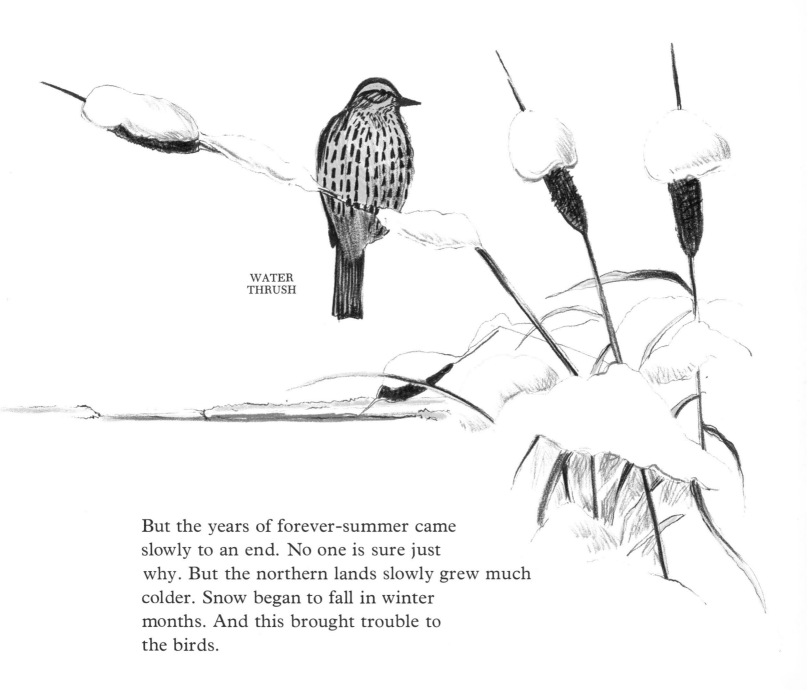

WATER
THRUSH

But the years of forever-summer came
slowly to an end. No one is sure just
why. But the northern lands slowly grew much
colder. Snow began to fall in winter
months. And this brought trouble to
the birds.

It took the climate thousands of years
to become colder. As the climate changed, the
birds had to change with it. They could
not think—but nature gives birds and other
animals strong feelings that they have to obey.
These mysterious feelings
help the birds in their lives.

YELLOW-BILLED
CUCKOO

MEADOWLARK

Cold weather killed some of the insects
and plants that the birds fed upon.
The birds had a strong feeling that they must fly
far away and look for other food.
Some birds flew north, where it was
still colder. These poor birds died.

YELLOW-BILLED
CUCKOO

Other birds flew south, where it
was warmer. They found more food
and they lived and had families.

YELLOW-BILLED
CUCKOO

When winter in the North was over, plants grew again and insects appeared. The birds slowly learned that they could return to their old homes in summer. It took thousands of years for them to learn this.

REDHEADED WOODPECKER

HUMMINGBIRD

As years went by, winters in the northland grew worse and worse. The great Ice Ages had come, bringing heavy snow and deep cold. Northern summers became very short and cool. But still some birds returned to nest.

LOON

Other birds flew farther and farther
south when cold weather came.
They looked for uncrowded places with
food. Some birds were strong enough
to cross the sea and go to South America.

PURPLE MARTIN

During the great Ice Ages, nearly half of North America was buried under ice caps called glaciers. No birds could live on these ice caps.

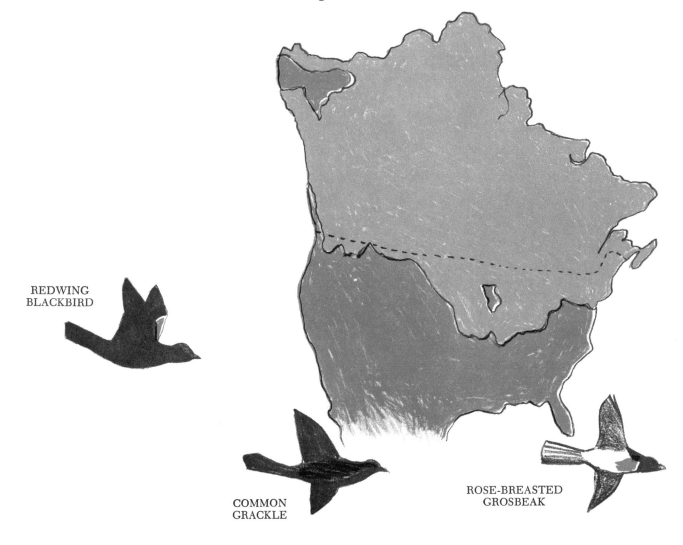

REDWING
BLACKBIRD

COMMON
GRACKLE

ROSE-BREASTED
GROSBEAK

NOWY
OWL

A few strong birds, able to stand
the cold, could still find food near
the edges of the glaciers.

ROCK
PTARMIGAN

Other birds had to go to the tropical southlands.
They could not stand the cold. But the
southern lands were already crowded with
tropical birds. It was not easy to find food.

GOLDFINCH

YELLOW
WARBLER

KINGBIRD

CUCKOO

REDWING
BLACKBIRD

When food is scarce, birds do not
have large families. They become
sick more often. Their numbers grow
fewer and fewer.

ROBIN

WREN

WOOD
THRUSH

BLUEBIRD

The great Ice Ages slowly came to an end. Little by little, the ice caps melted back. Each year, summer in the northland lasted a little longer.

ARCTIC TERN

The birds flew into these places
where the ice caps had been.
There was food there
for them in summer. They could nest
and raise larger families again.

GREAT BLUE HERON

When winter came, it was still
too cold to stay. So the birds
had to fly south, back to the crowded
southern land. But they did not
raise families in the South.

GREAT BLUE HERON

Instead, these traveling birds would
wait until spring and return to the
northland, where there was lots of
room and lots of food. There they would
lay their eggs in spring, and raise their
young in summer.

GREAT BLUE HERON

MALLARD DUCK

MALLARD DUCK

And when autumn came, the parent
birds and their grown-up young would
fly south together. There
the southern birds had raised
families while the visitors were gone.

Today we live at the very end of
the last great Ice Age. There are only
a few ice caps left, in Greenland and
Antarctica. Birds can be found in summer nearly
everywhere—even in northern Canada, Alaska, and
at the edges of Greenland.

WHISTLING SWAN

WHISTLING
SWAN

But the birds seemed to learn a lesson during
the great Ice Ages, and most of them have
kept the habit of traveling, or migrating,
to warmer lands when winter comes.

PURPLE MARTIN

Early in fall the days are still
warm. It seems much like summer
to most of us. But each morning
the sun comes up a little later.
Each evening it goes down a little
sooner.

HUMMINGBIRD

There is less light each day, and
this changes the birds' habits.
They have an urge to eat a lot and
grow fat. They must grow fat and strong,
because it will soon be time to migrate.

One night the smaller songbirds will begin to fly
away. Warblers, orioles, thrushes—they are mostly
birds that eat insects and fruit. Each night,
groups of them begin their flight to Mexico
and Central America.

The movements of the sun and stars in the sky tell them where they are, and how much farther they must go. Different kinds of birds go to different winter homes.

BLUEBIRD

WREN

Probably the birds go to winter homes
they lived in thousands of years ago,
during the great Ice Ages. Robins, wrens,
and bluebirds go to the southern
United States.

ROBIN

Purple martins travel in flocks of thousands. They go all the way to Brazil in South America. Bobolinks and swallows go even farther—to Argentina.

PURPLE
MARTIN

Swans, ducks, and wild geese fly
to the marshlands along the Gulf
of Mexico.

SWAN

BLUE
GOOSE

BLACK
DUCK

SNOW
GOOSE

Some birds do not migrate. There are those that stay in the southern lands all year around.

TOUCAN

Some northern birds stay all winter.
They are mostly those kinds that can
live on dried berries, seeds, and other
food that can be found above the snow.
Some hunting birds also stay behind.

GREAT
HORNED OWL

CROW

CARDINAL

The stay-at-home northern birds are probably the kinds that once lived at the edge of the ice cap during the great Ice Ages. They did not learn to migrate because they didn't have to.

CHESTNUT-COLLARED
LONGSPUR

SNOW BUNTING

BLUEBIRD

Each winter, the days keep getting
shorter until about December 21. Then
the days begin to get longer again.
Every day the sun rises a little earlier.
Every evening the sun sets a little later.
Spring is on its way.

WHITE-THROATED
SPARROW

CARDINAL

People who live in lands that have winter
are glad to see spring come each year.
And they are glad to welcome back the birds.